Words Given At The Well

Janice Kerr

Copyright ©2024 Janice Kerr
All rights reserved.
Published by Red Penguin Books
Bellerose Village, New York
Library of Congress Control Number: 2024905001
ISBN 978-1-63777-570-7

No part of this book may be reproduced in any form or by any electronic or mechanical means, including information storage and retrieval systems, without written permission from the author, except for the use of brief quotations in a book review.

Dedication

"Praise be to GOD and the Father of our Lord Jesus Christ, the all-merciful Father, the GOD whose consolation never fails us!
He comforts us in all our troubles, so that we in turn may be able to comfort others in any trouble of theirs and to share with them the consolation we ourselves receive from GOD."
(II Corinthians 1:3 and 4, NEB-version)

This book is dedicated to:
Suzanne Lewis-McNeil
and
Denise Edwards
Without their obedience to the above scripture, I would not have come to know of GOD's love and deliverance!

Special thanks

I want to give special thanks to Mimi Finnegan for selflessly giving of her editing expertise upon the inception of my book.
I am forever grateful for the time and efforts you so freely gave and provided!
Again special thanks!

Acknowledgments

I want first of all to take the time to thank GOD for all HE has done in my life and for giving me the strength and courage to write these expressions of HIS presence.

Secondly, I want to thank my husband for his never ending support and encouragement in all areas of my life. Without his strong stand with GOD, this project would not have come to fruition. I love you with all that I have!

To Cousin Bert and Joshua my captive audience, thank you for your support. I love you.

Richard DiBartolo, my illustrator, thank you for putting a visual comprehensive image to each poem ... I simply say on point.

Thank you to my pastor, Rev. John McCave, for his rightly-divided teachings which proved a catalyst to my understanding of the Bible—to this end, that GOD has used me as a vessel.

Preface

"Yahweh GOD, [is] merciful and gracious, longsuffering, and abundant in goodness and truth." (Exodus 34:6b, KJV)
As I live each day, I know this is true!

Not only did GOD save me with the gift of HIS son, HE continues to provide exceedingly abundantly above all I ask or think. (Ephesians 3:20)

GOD has healed my heart and mind from childhood wounds. GOD has given me a gift which could only be from HIM. I have never been a strong speller or reader, now HE has me writing poems!

These poems are divinely inspired. The ideas for the poems come while sitting in church, listening to GOD's word being taught. Most of the poems come from specific sections of scripture (which will be indicated).

The poems are also based on biblical understandings.

Each chapter has a theme expressed by a specific passage of scripture.

If one is willing, GOD will make HIMSELF known to that person in a uniquely individual way! Proving HIS care for you, HE will begin revealing your part in the perfecting of the saints and in drawing people near to HIM.

Table of Contents

Chapter 1 - GOD's Provision

Chapter 2 - A Proper Response

Chapter 3 - GOD Centered

Chapter 4 - Astray

Chapter 5 - Pondering My Household

Epilogue

Chapter One

GOD's Provision

Acts 5:39

Asunder

Two paths cross...
An innocent meeting...
A notice, a nod, or so we're thinking.
GOD's planned meeting!
A relationship forms, nuptials ensue, now two are one.
GOD' gift for you!
Past baggage reveals two wounded beyond measure.
GOD's plan is to fit them together.
Struggles of life attempting to swallow what has happened;
They allow the threefold cord to unravel.
Stop, and take notice of the schemes that are at play.
Go to GOD with meekness, and surrender that day!
"Let no man put asunder"...that means you too,
And let GOD reunite the gift HE has for you!

Giving Back

I'm giving back the reins I have wrongfully taken,
The leather straps my hands have been tugging!

Throughout these years, I have struggled to be
The ruler of my marriage, you see,
Ignoring the pronouncement uttered in Genesis chapter 3.

I'm giving back the straps to the single owner –
my husband of whom I'm talking.
The godly way to live is to trust and submit,
As stated in the fifth chapter of Ephesians, my mind must commit.

Don't get me wrong; I have something to offer,
But seen in GOD's Word, there is an order!

A bold stance of obedience to the Heavenly Father,
Allows one's spouse to have the honor and respect he is to take hold of.

I will give back the reins and live as one.
I will start being blessed until death do us part!

GOD's Definition

Don't let deep wounds of pain and hurt come to define you.
Let GOD define you – HIS love, HIS mercies, HIS grace.
GOD's word gives life!
GOD's word is all powerful!
GOD's word penetrates the uttermost parts of your being, your heart, and soul!
GOD's word changes the lives of those who are meek to hear and understand!
GOD defines you as someone to love!

GOD's Mercy Is Full

GOD's mercy is full upon those who adhere to HIS ways.
GOD's mercy is not defined in times of plenty —
the plenty of trouble or gladness.
GOD's mercy was provided on Calvary!
Accepting GOD's son, believing in the Hope, and standing
places you in the position to obtain GOD's mercy.
GOD's mercy is full upon those who adhere to HIS ways.

In Times of Old

It was spoken of in times of old
Of a savior I've been told,

Who would lay down His life, obediently!
But none took notice of Him, as the Anointed Christ you see.

He was spoken of as that "carpenter's son,"
The one who was said to have blasphemed, it had begun.

He spoke against the Pharisees,
Until they sought and hung Him from the tree.

It was spoken of in times of old
That He would be stricken and afflicted as the record foretold.

We must trust and believe and take hold
Of the PLANS that were spoken of in times of old.

Part II

Wait! There will be a part II, definitely!

Christ agreed for you and me
To take on the servant role, you see.

He accepted the shame of the judgments, accusations, and blame.
He endured what came out of being delivered unto death.

The beatings, railing, and sufferings had to be
To gain the glory of Christ, you see.

The sufferings of Christ were written as plain as can be
Throughout the Bible for all to see.

One must read the books of Moses, the prophets, and Psalms
To gain the knowledge of what GOD foretold.

In these books we can see,
The telling of part II, when Christ returns for you and me!

Part II is the realization of what Jesus proclaims
As the acceptable year and vengeance of Yahweh

When the Christ sits on the throne
And begins to wipe the tears of all those who mourn.

Part II is definitely coming, we must wait and stand
until the Christ returns again!

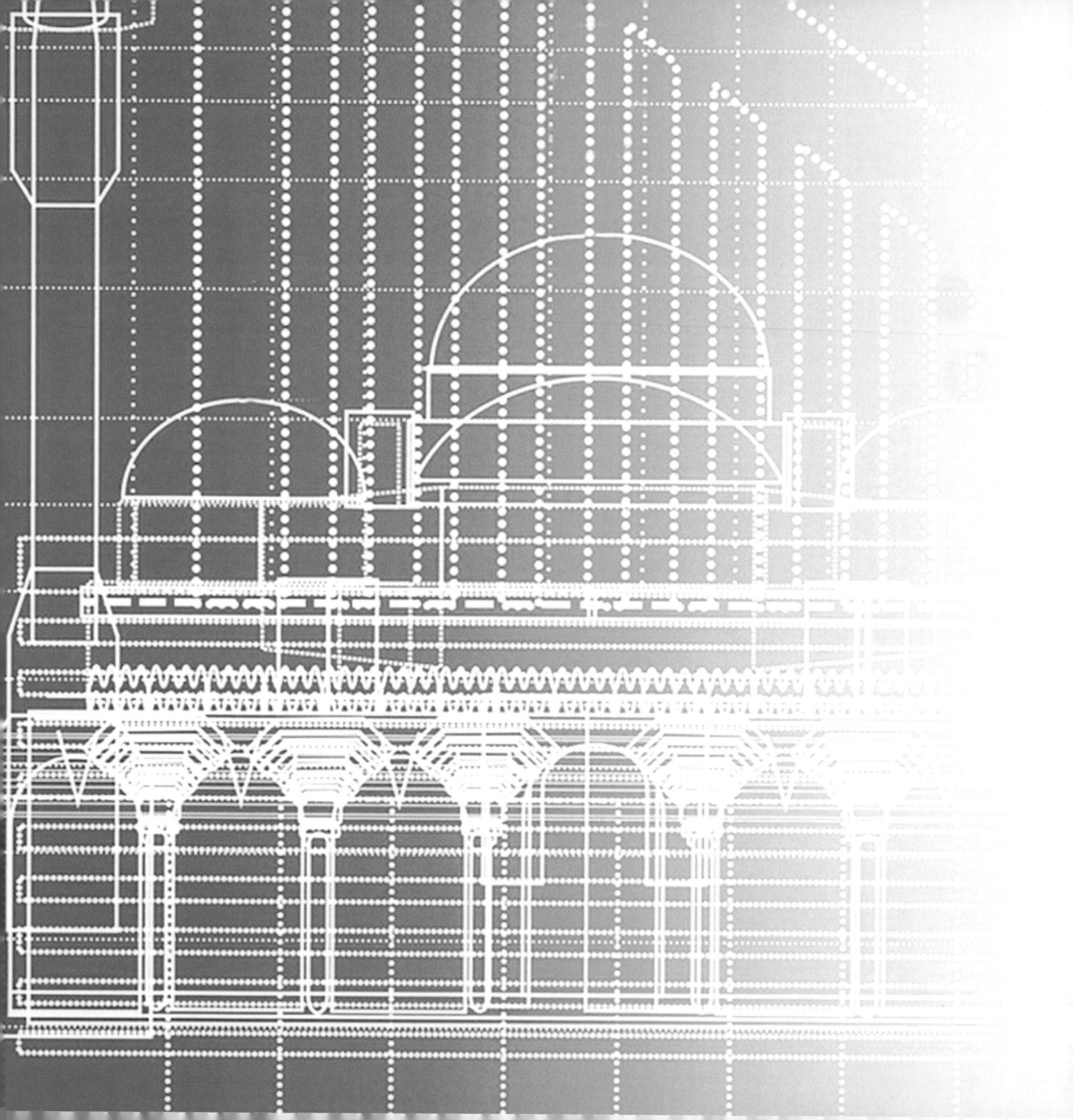

Planned Reconciliation

It began with a plan, a plan of reconciliation with HIS people.
It was planned for us!

The plan was carried out by HIS Christ.
The plan was carried out with the sacrifice of HIS son, Christ Jesus.
It was done for us!

Through that sacrifice, the division was broken down.
Two peoples were made ONE NEW BODY.
Now, both have access to the one true GOD.
It was designed for us!

For all who choose are reconciled unto GOD.
Enmity with GOD exists no more!
Reconciliation with GOD was planned for us!

Recipe

Cross

Humility

Reconciliation

Intercession

Sacrifice

Trespasses

GOD has given us the recipe for life!
Found in the Book of Life, on every page and
in the chapters from Genesis to Revelation.
The recipe must be followed to the tee, to enjoy GOD's eternity.
As you read the Book of Life, you will see the tee,
the main ingredient, is Christ!

The Law of Faith

The law of faith comes through Jesus the Christ, the son of GOD.
One way, one truth— GOD's way...
Believing GOD provided HIS son to take away our sins.
Not your work! GOD's work!
Not your way! GOD's way!
Take heed to GOD's provision!
Accept GOD's law of faith.

Chapter Two

A Proper Response

II Corinthians 5: 16-21

Courage to Fly

GOD has healed you through and through.
Take HIS hand, and let HIM lead you.
Your wings are now unhindered,
they are no longer clipped.
Let the plan of GOD endlessly equip.

But you have thoughts of inability, lies from the pit!
These thoughts attempt to control your cadence and
encourage you to quit.

You must hold on, stand, and learn to trust;
"Trust in the LORD with all your heart; and
lean not unto your own understanding.
In all your ways acknowledge HIM,
and HE shall direct your paths."

There may be bumps and curves, but stay the course,
And HE will show you, your own life's worth!

Divinely Healed

Having no more thoughts of being damaged goods…
I now know it is ok to love myself.
I am free indeed from hidden shame!
Free to shine like how I was made!

Shattered no more…
No need to only survive, in pieces of deceit and lies.
I am now exquisitely re-correlated by the hand of GOD!
Free to live life, to glorify!

I now have accepted to love myself.
I have the privilege to perform, my calling from GOD!

Enlightened Response

It is a precious gift to lead people to the GIVER.
A precious gift to lead people...
Those we love,
Those we meet,
Those we greet,
Those we connect with.
The choice is theirs, with my prayers.
My enlightened response is because of the precious gift that was given.
Because someone led me, I now have received the gift of reconciliation...
To lead with my life,
To lead with my words,
To lead with my acts,
For another to choose the GREATEST GIFT GIVER of all!

Gaze

With our gaze on others, we watch their actions and ways.
Upon that scrutiny of them, that watching and observing,
We seemingly elevate our walk with others' shortcomings.

We are unaware of what a deception!
The gaze made should be upon GOD's ways!
No self-elevation can be gained with that gaze!

Compare your walk to the true TEACHER'S ways,
and allow meekness to replace the deception of your horizontal gaze!

GOD Is Not Superman

GOD is not Superman; HE's so much better!
Remember this: "He's faster than a speeding bullet,
More powerful than a locomotive?
He leaps tall buildings in a single bound.
Look up at the sky. It's a bird; it's a plane. No! It's Superman!"
Tuning in and watching that TV show gave such a false sense that he, Superman,
had the power and strength to care and always be there, in your time of need,
whenever that may be.

Like I said, GOD is not Superman; HE's so much better!
First of all, HE is not a man that HE should lie with creative thoughts that beguile your mind.
Second of all, HIS words are true as seen in Colossians chapter 2.

Plainly written for me and for you.

If we dive into HIS word we can see what we have heard!
We can see with our eyes GOD's words on the pages telling us of HIS Son, our Lord and Savior.
Who died for our trespasses and sins! I'm just saying, what comfort that brings!

Third of all, GOD wants us to retain knowledge of HIS word,
to the end that we walk in what we've learned.
That is how our hearts may be encouraged, being knit together in love.

GOD is not Superman, in this we must trust, HE's so much better, because HE first loved us!

Help My Focus

Help me, oh GOD.
Help me to trust in YOU bigger than I do.
Help me during the day-to-day to walk in YOUR ways.
Help me to remember YOUR Son's focus…
Who when He was reviled, He reviled not.
His focus was fastened on YOU.
His heart and eyes focused on THE PRIZE.
Help me to trust in YOU bigger than I do.
Help me during the day-to-day to walk in YOUR ways
…so in THAT day I won't be ashamed of a lifetime of going astray!
I want to see the ONE who laid down His life for me!

How Long

How long, how long will it be?
That you continue to behave like an unwilling child toward me?
You say, "I know, I know," but do not do.
Where do you think that behavior will land you?
If you say you know my ways, why do you continually disobey?

Meekness is one of the qualities you must possess.
In Hebrews chapter 12 is a helpful example that shows how to do it best.
…Where does your focus lie?
…Chastening of my children.
…Reverence leads to life.
Read it for yourself, don't live a lie,
My words are written down to be your guide.
My words guide you into obedience, if you open your heart to see.
That behavior will land you in eternity with ME!

The Race

Christ, who is the finisher of our faith, has set the pace of the race.
An event we choose to enter ourselves in, to the end we want to win.
Yet, sometimes in life, we find that we have veered off course.
With things that laden our pace.

Yet, thanks be to GOD for HIS grace!

We must endure to run this race.
Ask GOD to help us with our focus.
So we can run with endurance, to finish the race that is set before us.

What I Want For You

What I want from you is humility.
What I want from you is honesty.
These two go together.
Without these two...
You won't know you need forgiveness.
You won't know you need my help.
You won't learn my words.
You won't gain what I want for you...MY ETERNITY!

Ye Of Little Faith

Ye of little faith…
GOD has provided.
GOD has supplied.
GOD has promised.
Ye of little faith…
Trust in GOD's provision.
Accept what GOD has supplied.
Stand on GOD's promises
Know that HIS words are true.
Ye of little faith…
Remember that GOD has provided.
Remember GOD has supplied.
Remember GOD has promised.
For if you remember…
your faith will be big enough to move mountains…
for you know GOD can!

Chapter Three

GOD Centered

Psalm 25

In GOD We Trust

GOD has allowed the opportunity for us to trust in HIM
With the induction of each newly-elected president,
a president that can be guided with the prayers and cries
    of GOD's children,
Those children who obey GOD's word,
Those children who remember GOD's word,
Those children who remember that GOD says…
"I will take care of MY people, I will take care of those that keep
their eyes, heart, and mind focused on ME, those who have
looked, heeded, and expected the promises of MY word."
GOD has allowed the opportunity for us to trust in HIM.

In Your Presence Is The Fullness Of Joy

In YOUR presence is fullness of joy.
What does that mean?
Hum, let's see...
"Fullness:" a hard word to remember the specific definition, in fact,
To me, it's a cerebral thought, a feeling, an act.
So what did I do? I looked it up, to put my finger on it, exact.
The word consists of an adjective with a suffix, that defines the
 state or the being of possessing: an abundant, complete,
sufficient amount of supply, it describes.
This word defined is starting to remind me of GOD, that I can't deny.
"Joy," on the other hand, is a feeling easily defined.
Thoughts that are provoked come straight to mind,
a birth, a wedding, and a long awaited reply.
Hey! Wait a minute, GOD is part of this definition too, I comply.
In YOUR presence is fullness of joy...I got to "think in"- it's a choice!
A choice to keep GOD with us day in and day out, to look to HIS
 proficiency, and not be led to doubt!

Some People Say

Some people say I'm Lucky

I say, "I have GOD's favor!"

Some people say, "The planets are aligned …"

I say, "GOD aligns my path!"

Some people say, "I hope that works out for you …"

I say, "My hope is in GOD's deliverance!"

I am GOD loved!

I am GOD regarded!

I am GOD led!

GOD blesses me! Does GOD bless you?

Kindness
LOVE
VIRTURE
Patience

Sure Election

How do we know our election is sure?
The answer is when one constantly engages in actions that are pure,
Pure in virtue, temperance, patience, kindness, and love,
And the knowledge of the words of our LORD above.
Diligent practice is the key of passage to gain entrance into
the dynasty of the LORD's eternity.
Let your faith be at work and with daily recall of the sin that was
purged for one and for all.

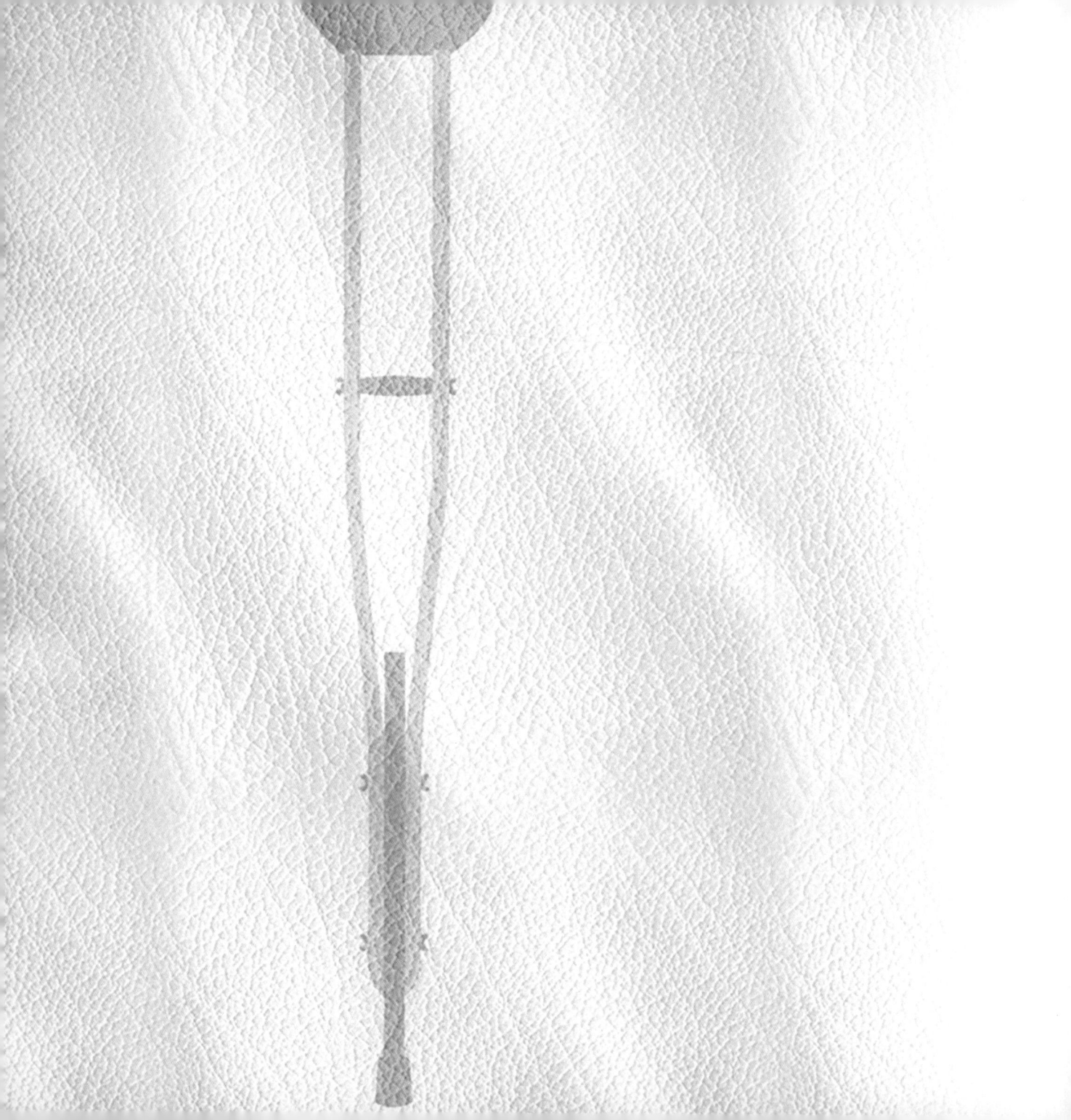

The Crutch

They say if one believes and trusts in GOD, that reliance spells crutch.
I say… so what! For I spell crutch this way.
Choice to choose the GIFT-GIVER.
Resist not evil.
Understanding the full knowledge of GOD's mercies.
Temperance in all things.
Courage to stand against the norm.
Heeding to the ways of GOD.
My crutch helps me through life's journey that is filled with trials, protecting what was injured by the fall!

The Hope Will Come

The Hope will come.
A peaceful patience must occur.
A steadfast endurance must occur.
Faithfulness must occur.
Endure the pain that happens while waiting for the Hope.
The Hope will come.
Wait, watch, hunger, study, and seek to endure to the coming of the Hope!

The Same Way

The same way He loved,
The same way He taught,
The same way He died,
We must incline our ways to,
Lead as He led.
Love as He loved.
Teach as He taught.
Die to ourselves as He did.
There is only one way to do it, the same way...
by allowing the indwelling of the paracelete to reign!

Chapter Four

Astray

Ephesians 2:1-10

Attributes of Love

Some people have attributes of love ...
They are patient.
They are kind.
They give their all at all times.
They are selfless.
They give their best.
They stop at nothing less.
They care without fear, but their actions will never come near
   to the price paid so dear!
It cannot even compare!
For without accepting what GOD provides,
these attributes above will be denied.
GOD sent HIS son as a gift, you see.
Paid with HIS life endearingly.
So that each, and all, who truly believes ...
can live eternally.
Those who believe have learned to love
from the example above.
They love, because HE first loved us!

IDOLATRY

Disobedience is the key to idolatry.
It is not a place we want to be!
Our defense can only be GOD's WORD,
HE has given to you and me.
Diligently we must be aware
Of the adversary's subtle schemes and snares!

Identify

Disobedience

Obstructing your

Loyalty;

Acknowledge

Totally any

Rebellion against

Yahweh!

Liberty in Christ

We have been granted liberty in Christ, you see.
The price was paid in full on Calvary.
We must believe in what He has accomplished for us,
And stand in the revelation of the gospel's worth!

But free indeed, cannot be free in me.
It leads me to believe in my own ways.
It leads me to believe in doctrines of men.
Rather than the exemption provided through HIM!

We must remember what GOD has taught in days of old,
And walk in faith for what our future holds.

Under God's Wings

Wings of iron have come to be, many people's saving grace, you see.
They trust solely in the people who govern,
instead of the ONE who is upholding.
Our country was founded on godly principles, you see.
The Founding Fathers knew what wings to seek!
GOD's wings are what we need.
With our prayers, HE works in the hearts of those who lead.
Wings of true strength and protection, HE provides.
In the shadow of HIS wings will I abide!

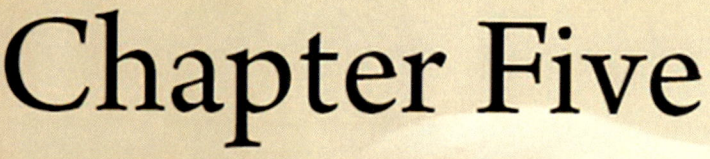

Chapter Five

Pondering My Household

Proverbs 31: 10-27

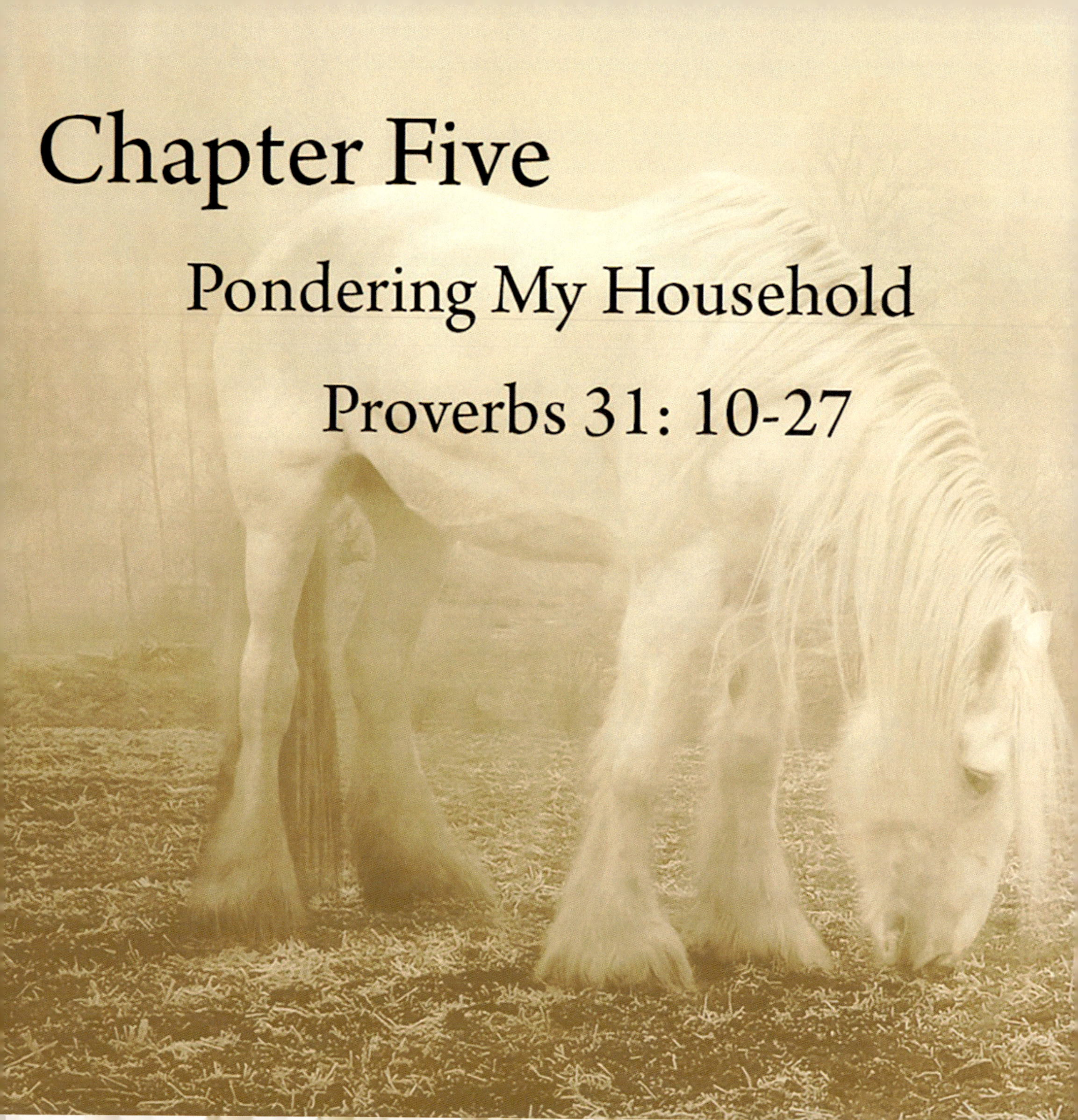

Know

I didn't know that June 29th would be a day of sorrow for my family and me.
I didn't know it would be a day we would lose a dear brother off the family tree.
I didn't know that May 24th could have been the last time I would hear him say
"I love you Jan-Lynne."
I didn't know that Sonya, Michael and Deb this date too would come to dread.
But what I do know — our days are not promised,
that in a blink of an eye our life can change and never be the same.
I do know that death is something that happens to all,
and we must be ready when our number is called.
"Ready for what?" you must be thinking in your head.
Ready for the trump of the just for you've heard it's been said:

First Thessalonians 4:16, 17, 18:

For the Lord himself shall descend from heaven with a shout,
with the voice of the archangel, and with the trump of GOD:
and the dead in Christ shall rise first.
Then we which are alive and remain
shall be caught up together with them in the clouds,
to meet the Lord in the air and so shall we ever be with the Lord.
Wherefore comfort one another with these words.

I know I must hope in being raised to life from death.
This is the readiness of which was said.
Do these words comfort you?
If they don't, you are as good as dead!

Love In His Eyes

GOD gave me a man who looks at me with love in his eyes.
GOD gave me a man who fought for me and his commitment.
GOD gave me a man who honors me.
GOD gave me a man who is true to me.
GOD gave me a man who cherishes me.
GOD gave me a man who holds me,
A man who holds me anchored to the GOD
    who saved me through the gift of HIS Son.

GOD gave me yet another gift...
The gift of a man who looks at me with love in his eyes.

My Mom

My mom had the characteristics of a soldier -
If you looked.
My mom taught me how to be a peace maker -
If you listened.
My mom taught me how to be faithful -
If you watched.
My mom taught when you fall you get up
and continue to walk -
If you saw.
Her love was consistent, quiet, and gentle,
covering all the hearts
that came in contact with her -
If you remember.
She loved -
If you looked,
Like a soldier ... a soldier of Christ.

Christ's love led her.
Will you let Christ's love lead you?

My Son

Hopes and dreams I have for my son.
Praying that each one gets done.

Frets and worries are never too far.
Trying not to anguish over parenting mistakes that may mar.

In this too, I must trust, trust in GOD's truths, and HE'll get it done.
HE promises in HIS word, HE will finish what HE's begun!
Reading HIS word to comfort my heart…
Praying each day is another great start…
Especially when it deals with someone so dear to my heart!

Praying that my son will walk with GOD in meekness.
Desiring that he will finish the race until they meet, face to face.

Thank You Much

A man of honor,
A man of truth,
Holding onto his commitment to cherish,
Thank you much for being that —
Man of honor,
Man of truth.
Waiting until I allow GOD to fix what's broken...
What's broken in me, that affects "we."
Thank you much for being that —
Man of honor,
Man of truth,
A man holding onto his commitment to cherish.

What Manner of Salutation

"Hi sweetie," she would say,
when she greeted you anytime of the day.
A salutation spoken from her heart,
I will miss that greeting for the time we are apart.
To survive this loss,
on these WORDS I will meditate:
... We shall be like him
... the dead shall be raised
... in the twinkling of an eye
... we shall be changed.
Seemingly to me, a big task it will be,
to comfort my heart,
For her death did us part.
My heart, GOD's word will mend,
until we meet again!

Epilogue

Chapter 1

Asunder - GOD designed marriage to bless us; with HIS help a marriage can remain a blessing. Get out of the way, let GOD ...

The Law of Faith - GOD has provided our salvation one way - GOD's way.

Planned Reconciliation - GOD has planned our reconciliation back to HIM since the fall in Genesis (3:15).

GOD's Mercy is Full - GOD is so merciful! GOD provided HIS Son; trust in that provision, and know the fullness of GOD's mercy.

GOD's Definition - When you believe GOD's Word, you allow GOD to define you and provide your real identity—HIS beloved child. This is not to be confused with your definition of yourself.

Recipe - GOD's Word provides you with the understanding of HIS provision of salvation through Christ Jesus.

Part II - This poem speaks of GOD's plan of the return and reign of HIS Son, Jesus the Christ.

Giving Back - This poem speaks on what I needed to learn in my marriage.

In Times of Old - This poem speaks about the foretelling of the Christ.

Chapter 2

An Enlightened Response - This poem came from thinking about two of my friends and my desire for them to be saved. (Update: one and her family have a relationship with GOD; I'm still praying for the other and his wife.)

Ye of Little Faith - This poem is about the pendulant struggles we as Christians have with our faith in GOD's provision.

Gaze - This poem speaks about how we as Christians tend to get distracted with the details of others' shortcomings, as a way to make ourselves feel better, instead of looking at GOD to elevate our walk.

Help MY Focus - This poem is a request to GOD to help keep one's walk righteous.

What I Want for You - This poem speaks on how to come to the knowledge of salvation from GOD's perspective.

How Long - This poem is a plea from GOD calling us to be obedient and reminding us that HIS Word will help us. GOD loves us and wants us to spend eternity with HIM.

The Race - This poem speaks on our focus and how it relates to standing on our faith.

GOD is Not Superman - This poem speaks about three things that are necessary to understanding the purpose of GOD's Word.

Courage to Fly - This poem is about once you've healed to keep your focus, thoughts, and trust upon GOD.

Divinely Healed - This poem speaks on the steps to follow after receiving healing from GOD.

Chapter 3

The Same Way - Our standard of living and loving has to come from the Christ's example. GOD has given us the Holy Spirit to accomplish our efforts.

The Hope Will Come - This poem speaks about our wait for the return of our Christ.

Some People Say - This poem speaks on our focus being a GOD centered one and knowing that GOD is present in our lives.

In GOD We Trust - This poem speaks on remembering that GOD upholds our lives and that we just need to go to HIM in prayer.

In Your Presence Is Fullness of Joy - This poem cleverly defines the choice to keep GOD as our focus.

The Crutch - This poem is one of my favorites. This poem puts a twist on an often heard negative comment that non-believers say to believers. This poem is also very special to me because, being in the field of physical therapy, I know how important a crutch can be!

Sure Election - This poem speaks about keeping your heart, mind, and soul stayed on the things of GOD.

Chapter 4

Attributes of Love - I wrote this poem about a friend who didn't seem interested in having a personal relationship with GOD. That friend possessed attributes but not the key ingredient.
Under GOD's Wings - This poem is about people who trust in man and not GOD.
Liberty in Christ - This poem doesn't mean freedom to believe and do whatever you want; rather, our freedom is in that which the "good news" provides.
Idolatry - This poem speaks on the hows and whats of idolatry.

Chapter 5

My Son - As parents, we wonder and fear if we are doing it right. We must take time to pray to GOD and relinquish our fears to HIM.
My Mom - After the death of my mom, as I was reflecting on her life, I became aware that she had the characteristics of a soldier of Christ.
Love in His Eyes - This is a reflection on my husband's committment to GOD which then can be felt and seen in how he honors our marriage.
Thank You Much - This portrays my thankfulness for my husband's long suffering in dealing with my past childhood wounds that affect our marriage and his committment to honoring our marriage.
Know - This poem was written one day after my brother fell asleep. It speaks on the importance of being in the state of readiness when death arrives.
What Manner of Salutation - This poem was written to honor Cousin Bert, a beloved member of my family. This poem speaks of the Bible verses that comfort one when someone dies.

About the Author

Janice Kerr was born, raised and currently lives on Long Island, New York Janice endeavors to walk righteously before her GOD, love and care for her family. Professionally, Janice has worked as a physical therapist assistant for 30 years. As of late Janice has answered the call to be a vessel in perfecting of the saints and drawing people near to her GOD through her GOD given gift of poetry.
Words Given At The Well is Janice's first poetry book.

www.ingramcontent.com/pod-product-compliance
Lightning Source LLC
Chambersburg PA
CBRC091453160426
43209CB00024B/1884